Introduction

The strength of women in our society has been the ever-present, but the often quiet engine that kept the country progressing -- from Revolutionary War nurses to pioneer women to the much-needed factory workers during World Wars I and II.

This book will introduce you to the not-so-quiet women who chose to step up and lead the way to create a legacy of organizations and ideas that still benefit the greater Miami Valley community and your lives to this day. It's important to understand that these women lived in a time when very few had more than high school education, did not work outside the home, and until 1920, could not even vote.

And yet, the women you will meet on these pages still had the intelligence and the desire to make their world better. They also understood that there was great power in their ability to build relationships with each other and join forces to make good things happen. They worked on things like voting rights for women, labor problems, urbanization issues, immigration, migration, and corruption in the government. Sound familiar? Guess what—all of these issues are still with us today!

One of the first things these women also did was to find a place where they could call home, a place to meet and work together and support one another. The beautiful and graceful building at 225 N. Ludlow Street still stands today. It is a testament to over 100 years of the dedicated members of the Dayton Woman's Club maintaining it for generations of empowered women (and men) to support one another and join forces to make things happen.

The Dayton Woman's Club is now The Woman's Club Foundation-a non-profit organization whose mission is to be once again the meeting place to empower and support those who want to lead and make a difference in our community. It's your turn in the world. What do you want to change?

Deb McNeff, President
The Dayton Woman's Club

Historian and Co-Author

BIOGRAPHY for MOLLIE E. HAUSER

Marie J. Kumler, beloved teacher and leader, in 1907, organized the eight existing literary clubs to become the Dayton Federation. John H. Patterson wisely felt the Federation members needed a clubhouse in which to meet together. Patterson consulted with Mrs. Kumler about the purchase of a mansion in a central location for all members.

They chose the Steele/Darst mansion in Dayton's downtown area. This lovely home, built around 1850 by Mr. Steele, was purchased and remodeled at the time of the Civil War by Mr. Darst. The Federation purchased the home in 1916. They, too, added to the house so young women could have a home close to the area in which they were employed. By 1959 the Club was so successful that the women added a ballroom, the final change made to this mansion.

The purpose of the Dayton Federation was to unite the Club members for self-improvement and service to our community, our state and our nation. Sadly the Federation no longer exists, but the purpose of our membership remains the same.

Mollie Hauser is a devoted member of the Dayton community. She has dedicated her life to service and education. She earned her teaching and professional writing certificate from Wright State University and was employed for 20 years as Assistant Director of both a local and national nonprofit physicians' organization. She also edited the newsletter for these groups.

She currently serves as historian for the Dayton Woman's Club. She joined the Dayton Woman's Club in 2003. She also served on the Board of the Woman's Club Foundation and in 2011 served as President for one year. In 2016 she chaired activities for the 100th Anniversary of the Dayton Woman's Club.

Mollie is dedicated to civic work, serving the past 18 years as a community volunteer. Prior to this time, and while fully employed, she was a founding member and secretary of the Montgomery County Historical Society Guild. She also served as President for the Board of the Dayton Metro Library, and at the Dayton Art Institute, where she assisted the Dayton Art Institute Library Archivist.

In 2002 she was elected to the Board of the Opera Guild of Dayton and served for ten years, twice as Recording Secretary of the Holiday Tables fund raiser. She also served on the Board of Directors as Managing Vice President of Special Events/ Hospitality and later of Marketing/ Communications.

As part of her service to the community, Mollie was asked to take the position of Treasurer for the Dayton Federation Marie J. Kumler Scholarship program and was elected Corresponding Secretary and then Recording Secretary of the Board of the Dayton Federation of Women's Clubs.

Mollie E. Hauser
Past President/ Historian
The Woman's Club of Dayton

Note by Co-Author

Part two is all about the Women's Club Movement. Women's Clubs gained popularity right after the Civil War. There were clubs in cities and towns across the United States, including Dayton. But why? Women have not always been allowed to work or participate in public life. But women wanted to contribute to our culture and their communities. The best way for them to do their part was to get together with other women, known as "networking." It's a way of working together to get things done.

There were many different clubs, such as book clubs, where women would read and gain literary knowledge. Others focused on art or music. Charitable clubs helped raise money for the poor. Political clubs were formed to learn about politics and help change laws. Club members gathered at meetings to give reports on what they had learned and to come up with plans to make a difference in the community.

In Dayton, African American women formed the first women's club. It was called the Colored Literary Society, founded in 1884. Most of the history of women's clubs in the United States indicates that white, well-to-do women ran them. However, in Dayton, there were not only black women's clubs, but also clubs with black, white, and immigrant women, who together to accomplish great things.

Because of the literary clubs, women were inspired to form the Dayton Public Library. Similarly, the women of the Dayton Music Club helped to establish the Dayton Philharmonic Orchestra. And there would be no Dayton Art Institute if it weren't for women's clubs, which promoted a love of art in the community.

Having a strong network is critical to achieving goals. The women's clubs knew they had to support one another and work together to make their communities better. The women's clubs were essential to the founding of important cultural institutions in Dayton. More importantly, women's clubs paved the way for the passage of suffrage and equal rights within Dayton and communities across the entire nation.

Sherri Lynn Goudy, MH.
Historian/Marketing Coordinator
Children's Historical Publishing

Table of Contents

Part One

Dayton Women Influence History

Part Two

History of Dayton Women's Clubs

Part Three

Dayton Trailblazers in Women's History

Part Four

Test Your Knowledge

Electra Collins Doren

Each time you visit one of our library branches, you should thank a lady named Electra C. Doren. Imagine this – she began working for the Montgomery County Library when she was 18 years old and a few years later a library was named in her honor—The Electra C. Doren branch located on Troy Street close to Dayton Children's Hospital. Miss Doren was a loving friend to each of her library staff members. She approached problems in a new way establishing what today is the bookmobile for Daytonians who are unable to visit one of the library branches.

Doren believed in the importance of a woman's right to vote. She helped preserve its history with her large collection of papers of this movement. Ms. Doren helped found the League of Women Voters of Dayton that was formed in 1920.

In 1997, Electra C. Doren was inducted into Dayton's Walk of Fame, and in 1999, she was inducted into the Ohio Women's Hall of Fame.

Mary Davies Steele

Reading is a wonderful hobby. Today you can belong to a book club, or you can ask a group of friends to make plans for one of your own.

In 1889, Mary Davies Steele helped promote Dayton's very first book club, The Woman's Literary Club. Because of Mary's knowledge and love for books, she helped suggest the Club's programs for its first year.

Not only did Mary enjoy reading, but she also enjoyed putting her thoughts in writing. Some of her articles were published in the magazines of her day. She wrote articles for the local newspapers to express her interest in Dayton's public affairs, for she had true civic pride in her city. Mary also authored two books, one on the early life of Dayton, and one on living a happy life.

We, as historians, do not have a picture of this lady, sometimes shrouded in mystery. We must remember that Mary Davies Steele was an invalid, that she seldom left her room. The focus of her life was to care for other people and to lead a happy life. She wrote: "The heart at leisure from itself is the happy heart."

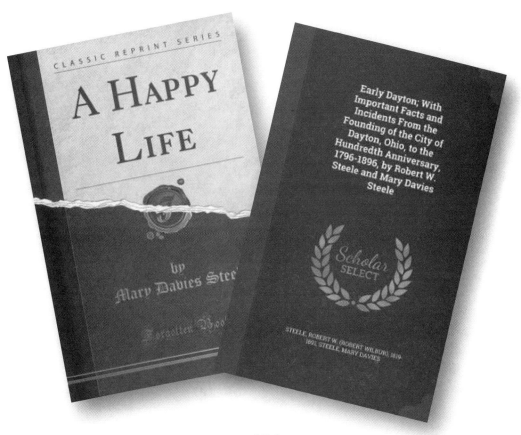

Dr. Gertrude Felker

Dr. Gertrude Felker was one of the first women physicians to practice medicine in the Dayton Area. In fact, in 1903 she and her business partner, Dr. Elenora Everhard, were among the first women doctors in the nation when they came to Dayton.

At the urging of a female college graduate, by 1907 Dr. Felker was working to establish an organization, College Women's Club. The purpose of this club was to bring together college graduates to encourage young women to further their education and to give volunteer service in the community.

In addition to her work as a physician and organizer in the College Women's Club and the Dayton Woman's Club, Dr. Felker was a leader in public health education. She headed a "clean up campaign" so that young people could have clean milk to drink. For her work, Dr. Felker was named "Woman of the Year" in 1954 and thus saved the lives of many children.

ORIGINAL CWC MEMBERS

Beedeker, (first name not recorded)
Clatworthy, Linda
Clements, Mrs. Frank
Everhard, Elenora
Felker, Gertrude
Fouts, Mrs. D. H.
Farman, Sue
Geyer, Emma
Gilbert, Mrs. Jessie
Greene, Grace A.
Hughes, Mrs. Flora L.
Kittredge, Mrs. Lyndon
Kumler, Mrs. F. A. Z.
LaRue, Mrs. Charlotte
Loos, Louise
Macke, Marcella
May, Mrs. W. C.
McCampbell, Nellie
McCord, Mrs. H. M.
McFadden, Cora

McKinley, Emma
McKinney, Effie
Miller, Mrs. L. K.
Drury, Mrs. W. A.
Pagenstecher, Clara
Rinehart, Pearl
Rotterman, Marie
Ryder, Winifred
Sapp, Donna
Schultz, Hattie
Spitler, Alice
Stephens, Mrs, Justina
Swadener, Blanche
Thompson, Bessie
Ward, Mrs. W. E.
Weaver, Mina J.
Wolpert, Maude
Wright, Katherine
Wuichet, Frances

Julia Shaw Carnell

Julia Shaw Carnell (1863-1944) promised to construct a new art museum for the city of Dayton if the community would pay for its operations. The challenge was met, and Mrs. Carnell donated nearly $2 million, a very significant gift on the eve of the Great Depression. The Dayton Art Institute's new building was completed in 1930 reflecting the Italian Renaissance style. The structure of nearly 60,000 square feet was designed by architect Edward B. Green of Buffalo New York. Once it was finished the Dayton Art Institute on its prominent hilltop location became known as "Dayton's living room," and people of all kinds visited to admire the extensive collection, take art classes in the Art Institute school, or enjoy the gardens. Mrs. Carnell's architectural gift to the city as well as the many artworks she donated to the museum continue to be enjoyed by present generations.—Inducted: 1996

Evangeline Lindsley

Can you imagine what changes in your world there will be 100 years from the day you are born? Evangeline Lindsley lived for 105 years. When she was born there were no computers, no cell phones, no airplanes, and nationally women had not been given the right to vote.

In 1996 at age 100, Ms. Lindsley wrote her story, "My Century: An Outspoken Memoir." She wrote of life in the 1900s: Dayton buildings that no longer exist, a time of horse and buggy, the first time she voted. Ms. Lindsley chose to be a teacher and was devoted to her students and a better life for all children.

After 46 years of teaching, she retired and began a life of volunteering. She worked with runaway children who were often pushed out of their own homes. Because she cared so much about the future of young people, she co-founded Daybreak in 1975 as an emergency shelter for runaway and homeless youth. Daybreak gives young people skills for an independent life style. The founding of this organization was one of Ms. Lindsley's outstanding contributions to the troubled youth, not only of Dayton but throughout the United States.

Evangeline Lindsley was inducted into the Dayton Hall of Fame in 1998.

Women's Right To Vote

In 1868, the 14th Amendment to the United States Constitution gave men who were U. S. citizens the right to vote for candidates for political office. Most men and even some women were positively against women's right to vote. Nevertheless many women, who called themselves suffragists, spoke out for their rights. Finally in 1920, the 19th Amendment to the Constitution was passed permitting American women the right to vote, a right known as women's suffrage.

In that same year, The League of Women Voters of the Greater Dayton Area was founded. Guided by Minnie Stanley the League members realized that most women did not understand how to vote. Mrs. Stanley organized a training program for these new voters. Today the League's objective is the same as it was—to educate the public concerning current events and politicians' beliefs in government principles.

Charlotte Reeve Conover

The Flood of 1913 washed away a significant amount of Dayton's history. Our city's citizens should give praise to a most respected local historian—Charlotte Reeve Conover.

Before her first book, The Flood published in 1907, Mrs. Conover interviewed both Mary Davies Steele and her father Robert for her book titled: "Some Dayton Saints and Prophets." So important were they that she devoted two parts to Robert and Mary Steele . She also wrote of some of Dayton's outstanding pioneers: author Paul Laurence Dunbar, business leader David L. Rike, and educators Captain Charles B. Stivers and David A. Sinclair.

Mrs. Conover was a leader in the Woman's Suffrage Party of Montgomery County. In an address before the Woman Suffrage Association, she spoke of the need for women to understand that the right to vote was important for the equality of women and men.

In "Dayton, Ohio - An Intimate History" published in 1932, Mrs. Conover wrote about the Women's Club Movement and the influence of such women as Mary Davies Steele, Electra Doren, and Marie J. Kumler who are included in this book .

In 2007 Mrs. Conover was inducted into Dayton's Walk of Fame.

A Clubhouse for Women

Have you ever been to a clubhouse or had one of your own? If you have, then you know how important it is. It's a place to meet with friends and only members can go there. The Dayton Woman's Club actually began as a clubhouse. It was a meeting place for the Dayton Federation of Women's Clubs.

Dayton Woman's Club, 225 North Ludlow Street

But where did they meet? The mansion at 225 North Ludlow Street, which still stands today, is one of the oldest residences in Dayton! It was built in the late 1840s by Robert W. Steele. His daughter Mary Davies Steele went on to help organize one of the first women's clubs, and she was very important to all of the women's clubs in Dayton.

After the Civil War, the new owner of the home, Napoleon Bonaparte Darst, remodeled it and added a third story to the building. During the Civil War the Darst Family supported the Union that was against slavery. Mrs. Dart added a wooden carving of an Eagle to the home, which was a symbol of patriotic allegiance to the Union. This beautiful Eagle can still be seen in the home.

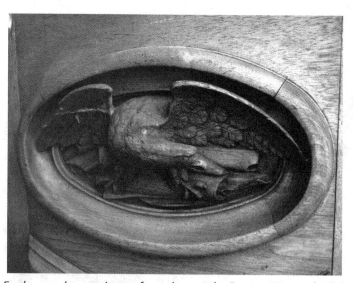

Eagle, wooden carving on front door at the Dayton Woman's Club

Fortunately, the historic mansion survived the Great Flood of 1913. And in 1916, the home was for sale. The women's clubs had no central location for their meetings. One of Dayton's most prominent citizens, John H. Patterson, urged his sister Julia to help the women of Dayton purchase a mansion that was still in good shape after the flood.

Many of the women's clubs joined together to purchase stock and come up with $5,000 needed for a down payment on the house.

On November 1, 1916 the club was officially incorporated, calling itself the "Woman's Clubhouse Company of Dayton, Ohio." Today it is simply called the Dayton Woman's Club. Their members are still active in helping the community and preserving the house for generations to come.

Tea Room at Dayton Woman's Club, 1918

The Plant, Flower, and Fruit Guild luncheon at the Dayton Woman's Club

Marie J. Kumler

Marie J. Kumler, known as the Mother of Clubs, was a beloved teacher and a leader among women in Dayton in the early 1900's. In 1907 under her guidance, eight women's clubs joined to form the Dayton Federation of Women's Clubs. Mrs. Kumler was elected as the first president of the Dayton Federation.

Because of her great interest in the welfare of young women, in 1908, the Dayton Federation began its most enduring project, the Marie J. Kumler Scholarship Loan Fund. This fund provided

Marie J Kumler

interest-free loans to young women for higher education. In later years the requirement was changed from women only to include worthy young men who needed help completing their college education.

In 1916 Mrs. Kumler became a founding member and the first President of the Dayton Woman's Club House Company. Under her guidance the Dayton Federation of Women's Clubs purchased the Club House at 225 North Ludlow Street.

In 2016 this Club celebrated 100 years of continuous service to the women of Dayton giving them a place for meeting with friends, for furthering education, and for philanthropic activities for the enrichment of the citizens of our city.

Clubs for Every Interest

The club movement in Dayton, Ohio, officially began in the 1880s. Some historians have written that the first club was the *Woman's Literary Club* in 1889. However, historic documentation shows that women in the African-American community started the *Colored Reading Room* in 1884. And the *Mozart Club*, which was a women's music club, began in 1888. It is clear that women in Dayton wanted to better their own lives and help their communities to become better as well.

By 1900, there were over 30 women's clubs in Dayton. There was a club for every interest you could think of, including literature, music, drama, business, welfare, gardening and science. The number of clubs continued to rise, as well as the number of women in the clubs. The first clubs initially formed with memberships limited to 20 or 30 women. But as more women wanted to participate, club membership expanded to include sometimes over 100 women, and men too!

Who recorded this information? One woman, who was a member of the *Woman's Literary Club*, became one of Dayton's most notable historians and authors. Her name was Charlotte Reeve Conover. She was a member and leader in several of the women's clubs in Dayton. By participating in these clubs, women found their strengths and talents and shared them with the community. They became leaders and discovered their voice by working together.

Hallie Q. Brown and female students at Wilberforce College

The Dayton Federation of Women's Clubs

By the early 1900s, there were many women's clubs active in Dayton, including clubs for literature, music, and art. Certain clubs helped workers improve conditions in factories. And other clubs focused on women and minorities seeking equality. All the clubs knew of each other, and some women were members of more than one. One goal that all the clubs had in common was to learn and to make their community better.

In 1907, Marie J Kumler had a big idea. Other cities across the U.S. had successfully joined forces to work together. This uniting, called "federating," was helping women in other towns improve their neighborhoods. If it was good enough for other places in the nation, then it was good enough for Dayton. The Dayton Federation of Women's Clubs, or DFWC came to be in 1907. Marie J Kumler was its first President. The DFWC's work was valuable and far-reaching to the history of Dayton.

Marie J Kumler

The DFWC had a substantial scholarship program that helped give money to young women wanting to go to college. The women of the clubs raised all the scholarship money themselves. Marie J Kumler was in charge of the program, and it was named after her. This scholarship program still helps women today!

One of DFWC'S most important decisions was to have a clubhouse. The DFWC didn't have a place to meet regularly, and after the 1913 flood many buildings and meeting places were destroyed. But the old Darst mansion was for sale, and with the help of John H. Patterson, the DFWC was able to buy it.

It became the Dayton Woman's Clubhouse. In this beautiful Victorian mansion, the women's clubs of Dayton came together to make their community better and to improve their own lives. And you can still enjoy the wonderful setting and activities of the club today.

Clubs to Serve the Community

As the club movement increased in popularity, club goals began to change. Clubs that once focused on educating themselves and their community shifted to concentrating on charity and community service. They promoted donations, fundraisers, scholarships and lunches for people in need.

Marie J Kumler center, seated at desk surrounded by board members of Young Women's League

One of the clubs focused only on community service was the Young Women's League. This organization began in 1898. They had a lunchroom, dorm, reading room and even a camp for young working girls and women.

Some of the civic clubs continue to be active today. The Junior League had its first meeting at the Dayton Woman's Club in 1919. Katharine Kennedy Brown was its first President and under her leadership they provided aid to families, children, hospitals and museums. Today, their programming includes a Girl Power Workshop that helps girls improve their self-esteem. The Christ Child Society of Dayton was founded in 1911. They provided aid to poor children, giving them clothes and toys during the holidays.

Racism and segregation led to struggles for black Americans in Dayton, such as educating their children and themselves and working at various jobs. African-American women often formed their own clubs to serve the community.

African-American organizations such as The West Side Day Nursery, founded in 1918, provided free daycare for working families. The black Women's Christian Association (WCA) No. 2, which would later become the Young Women's Christian Association (YWCA), was founded in 1889 by Louise Troy, Jessie Hathcock, Mary Shaw, and several others in the basement of the Eaker Street AME Church.

Mary Shaw, co-founder of the YWCA

Coming Together to Uplift the Community

Dayton's history seems to demonstrate something uncommon in the United States at the turn of the 20th century. Though racial discrimination still existed, a strong relationship, some may even call an alliance, developed between white and black activists.

Girls at the YWCA

The YMCA and YWCA were important groups in the community for education and social reforms. Founded in 1870, the YWCA in Dayton stands today as the oldest women's organization in the city and one of the oldest in the nation.

In 1889, Jewelia Higgins was one of the founding members of the black YWCA in Dayton. It was the first YWCA for African-American women in the United States.

The organization did not remain segregated for long. By 1932, the groups unified, and Mabel Evans became the first African-American on the Board of Directors. Today, one of the Dayton YWCA's primary goals is to provide programming and advocate for racial justice and civil rights.

The National Association for the Advancement of Colored People (NAACP) is the oldest and most recognized civil rights organization in the United States. It was established in 1909 by black and white activists, who wanted to see an end to the violence against people of color.

On February 9, 1915, the Dayton chapter of the NAACP was established. Lousie M. Troy, a black woman, and Julia Shaw Carnell, a white philanthropist, were among its founding members and leaders.

Today, the NAACP is one of the oldest surviving organizations in Dayton, which prides itself on being a multiracial, multinational, multicultural activist group dedicated to fighting social injustice for ALL in the community.

Louise Troy and Julia Shaw Carnell

Clubs Act During World War I

World War I coincided with the women's club movement. In Dayton, the clubs played a major role in contributing to the war effort. When the war began, women immediately mobilized to provide aid and support.

Women enlisted as nurses, despite being met with inequality and denied full enlistment opportunities in the U.S. armed forces. Many women also joined the Red Cross, which grew much larger during the First World War because of their participation. Jewelia Higgins of Dayton was the nation's first African-American Red Cross nurse.

The YWCA was an important institution for the war effort as well. In fact, the YWCA was the only women's organization that served as part of the WWI campaign, providing volunteers and workers overseas. Black women joined the YWCA increasingly during WWI to meet the specific needs of black soldiers.

Just before the outbreak of WWI, Marie J. Kumler, the mother of the clubs, united the many Dayton women's clubs into an umbrella organization called the Dayton Federation of Women's Clubs.

The women united under the Federation in Dayton contributed to the war effort, while still retaining their other club goals. The organization was a driving force for war relief in 1918. Their annual report of the work they accomplished from 1918-1919 reveals how. Not only did they prioritize war efforts, but they also became more organized and efficient, and maintained their existing literary programs.

The Dayton Woman's Club Gives Back

The Dayton Woman's Club was started as a clubhouse for all the women's clubs of Dayton to have a place to meet. Eventually, the clubhouse became its own club. The mission of the club was to maintain the historic house, to be open to the community, and to serve the community through philanthropic endeavors.

What is a "philanthropic endeavor?" It is the act of giving, often money, to help people in need. The Dayton Woman's Club gave money to the community for various projects in the 1930s and 1940s. Donations included giving $200 for the band shell at Island Park, which would equal about $3,500 today! The band shell was an amazing venue where people would go picnic and hear a concert performed by the Dayton Municipal Band or a famous band or musician.

Another way to give back to the community is by donating your time and talents. The Dayton Woman's Club gave back during World War I and World War II by sewing items soldiers needed. The sewing club met once a week and donated their items to the Red Cross.

The Dayton Woman's Club continued to give to the community until the 1950s when money became tight, and they had to repair the roof of the house. It seemed after that time, there was always something wrong with the aging home with very little money left to help the community.

But now, the situation is changing. The club now has a member who is totally devoted to philanthropy. Today, the club gives money to Artemis and the YWCA to help women and children in the community. They give toys and also support the Book Fair Foundation.

Why Did Women's Clubs Help the Community?

The women's club movement happened during a time of great change in the United States. The Industrial Revolution was underway, and the construction of new factories caused populations to rise. How? The new factories created jobs, which caused people to move to the cities in large numbers.

John H. Patterson

In Dayton, one such factory was the National Cash Register Company known as NCR. . Its founder and president, John H. Patterson, was a big supporter of the women's clubs in Dayton. But why?

Dayton and other cities were becoming crowded with new people looking for jobs. There were poor conditions in the city, and the women's clubs thought they could help improve people's lives. Because many of them were middle-class women who did not work, they had the time and resources to devote to such a cause. Patterson backed the clubs 100 percent.

The Dayton Daily News published an article written by Patterson in 1901. He said, "The future betterment of conditions in this country depends largely upon what the women will do. Women are fearless in support of their ideals and have the time to devote."

Patterson was an important man in Dayton. People in the community listened to him because of his wealth and influence. He used his position of power to help the women's clubs, especially financially. He gave many clubs money to help them get started, including the Dayton Women's Club.

John H. Patterson (right) with family

Suffrage: Getting the Right to Vote

In 2020, the nation will celebrate the 100th anniversary of women's suffrage in the United States. Ohio was one of the first states to make it law, or "ratify" the

19th Amendment for women's suffrage, the right to vote. Official ratification by the entire nation occurred on August 26, 1920.

But gaining the right to vote in 1920 was not the beginning of the story. Women in Dayton had been fighting for the right to vote since 1869 when the first women's suffrage association was formed.

This group only lasted a few years, and another association was formed in the late 1880s, which also disbanded. It seemed there was not enough support in Dayton for a suffrage club to exist. Finally, in 1912, the Dayton Woman Suffrage Association of Montgomery County (also called the DWSA) was formed and remained.

The leaders of the DWSA included women who were already active in the women's club movement, including the founder and president Jesse Leech Davisson. The success of these clubs was because of women's willingness to "network," which is why women were members of multiple clubs.

Women's League for African American Suffrage, 1899

Marching for the Right to Vote

The DWSA succeeded in getting the public to support their fight for the vote by holding marches and parades. One major parade happened on October 24, 1914, and marchers included the famous Wright family. Orville and his father Milton marched alongside Katharine Wright, who was a member of the DWSA.

The DWSA also had famous speakers come to Dayton and speak about suffrage. This included suffragette Carrie Chapman Catt who spoke just three days before the October 1914 parade.

Catt spoke about the facts regarding women's suffrage and how it would help the entire nation, not just women. The speaking engagement was in preparation for the November 3, 1914 election when the women's suffrage issue was on the Ohio ballot. However, it was a risky topic, and a majority of Dayton men defeated the women's suffrage issue in the voting.

*Katharine, Orville, and Milton Wright
photographed with other family in 1915*

Working Together for the Right to Vote

The DWSA gained great support by cooperating with black, immigrant and working-class women. Other cities in Ohio and the U.S. focused only on white, middle or upper-class women getting the right to vote. Dayton women realized they needed to all work together to achieve their goal.

Jewelia Higgins and Hallie Q. Brown were two leaders within the African-American community who worked alongside Jesse Davisson and other women of the DWSA. Some of the women who spoke Hungarian and German were able to reach out to the immigrant population for support. The DWSA also gave speeches at NCR to appeal to the working women in the factory.

Men such as John H. Patterson supported women gaining the right to vote and having a political voice in the community. Just as he had done for the women's clubs, Patterson contributed money to the DWSA. In telegrams from 1912, he wrote, "woman's suffrage is right and, in the end, must win," as well as, "woman's suffrage is America's greatest opportunity for...betterment."

Working together, or "networking," is extremely important to build momentum for a cause. In this case, by 1919, a majority of Dayton citizens were finally in support of women having the right to vote.

Jewelia Higgins

Hallie Q Brown

The League of Women Voters

Although the passage of the 19th Amendment was a monumental success for women's rights, not all women exercised their new right to vote. Why? Some women didn't vote because they didn't have knowledge about the politics or issues of the day. What could be done to change this lack of understanding? The new goal for women's political clubs was to educate women about citizenship.

In Dayton, The League of Women Voters was formed out of the existing members of the DWSA. Under the new leadership of Minnie Stanley, the League organized classes to help women learn how to vote and understand what issues were on the ballot.

Another community member, Annie McCully, helped teach classes as well. Just like other women in the club movement, McCully was involved in other clubs as well, and she was Dayton's first policewoman.

The League was a major force in improving the city of Dayton. They helped women learn about issues and political candidates by publishing a newsletter. They also helped revise the school code of Ohio, resulting in the schooling of 17,000 children who had previously been deprived of an education. The League of Women Voters still works today with the same goal of educating the public about political issues and events.

Katharine Kennedy Brown, voting for the first time

The Bush Family Connection

Many of the women written about in this book are probably not names you have heard of before. Though they accomplished great things, ordinary citizens are not often recognized for the extraordinary things they've done to make life better for all of us.

However, there is a famous family from Dayton that you may recognize. Former First Lady Barbara Bush had strong family ties to Dayton. Her grandparents were residents of Dayton, and Mrs. Bush would often visit them in the summer, traveling from New York by train with her father. Her father was overseeing construction of the McCall Publishing plant in Dayton, and later became President of the company. Both of her grandparents

Mabel Pierce, Grandmother of former First Lady Barbara Bush

accomplished great things in Dayton as well. Her grandfather, Scott Pierce, was one of the founders of the Dayton Rotary Club. And her grandmother clearly influenced young Barbara.

Mabel Pierce was very active in the community. She was a member of the Dayton Woman's Club in 1920. From 1921-1923, Mabel served as president of the Women's Literary Club. More than likely, she inspired a love of reading in her granddaughter Barbara Bush, who supported reading and literacy programs as First Lady of the United States. Mabel also served as president of the Dayton Federation of Women's Clubs. Along with the other leaders of the DFWC, Mabel united the more than 5,000 club members of Dayton in their work.

What's Inside the Clubhouse?

The Dayton Woman's Clubhouse is one of Dayton's oldest residences. The clubhouse was built in the late 1840s, and it survived wars and the 1913 flood. When all other residences in its original neighborhood were demolished, it survived. And because of the Dayton Woman's Club, and the financial support of the founding women and John H. Patterson, the clubhouse has still survived.

What does it look like inside this beautiful three-story mansion? One of the first features that captures your eyes is the fancy hand-carved wood trim. There are imported white marble fireplaces in the parlor and sitting room. A hand-carved wooden Eagle sits proudly in the house, a symbol of freedom and the Union during the Civil War. The rooms are elegantly furnished with antique and replica furniture that reflects the 19th century. The staircase to the second and third floor is also finely carved and lit from a skylight.

In the hallway, beside the staircase, is a grand Italian-style fountain. The fountain was installed by the clubwomen in the 1920s. It is made of "Rookwood" tile, which was a famous ceramic company in Cincinnati. The company is over 130 years old and still manufactures tile and other ceramics today!

In the rear of the house are the ballroom and entertainment areas, where the award-winning garden once lived. The clubhouse is a beautiful place to visit, and the clubwomen are definitely fulfilling their mission to care for the home. They take great pride in sharing it with the community and decorating it wonderfully for holidays and special occasions.

It became the Dayton Woman's Clubhouse. In this beautiful Victorian mansion, the women's clubs of Dayton came together to make their community better and to improve their own lives. And you can still enjoy the wonderful setting and activities of the club today.

Part Three:
Dayton Trailblazers in Women's History...

1867—Emma L. Miller was the first federal woman employee in what today is known as the Department of Veterans Affairs. She was also the first woman and only civilian in U.S. history to be laid to rest with full military honors.

1869—The first women's suffrage association formed in Dayton.

1879—Electra C. Doren became the library director of the Dayton Library system.

1884—The first African-American women's organization, "The Colored Reading Room," was formed in Dayton, led by Capitola Douglass, Lula Henderson, Emma Sherman, Mary Sloan and Louisa Troy.

1887—Hallie Q. Brown was the first Black woman to earn a Master of Science degree from Wilberforce University.

1889—The first women's literary club was formed in Dayton by Mary Steele.

1989—The Young Woman's League of Dayton was formed by Marie J. Kumler.

1903—Jane Reece opened her Dayton studio; she was a highly acclaimed American pictorial photographer and one of Dayton's most prominent artists.

1906—Dayton's first female physicians, Dr. Gertrude Felker and Dr. Elenora Everhard, helped form the College Women's Club in Dayton.

1907—Marie J. Kumler organized the Dayton Federation of Women's Clubs.

1912—Dayton Woman Suffrage Association of Montgomery County was formed and led by Jesse Leech Davisson.

1914—Annie McCully became Dayton's first policewoman.

1915—Lousie Troy and Julia Shaw Patterson Carnell helped found the Dayton Chapter of the NAACP

1917-1918—Jewelia Higgins was Dayton's first Black Red Cross nurse, and she helped found Dayton's first YWCA for Black women.

1919—Annae Barney Gorman founded the Barney Community Center, now known as the Children's Medical Center of Dayton.

1921—League of Colored Women Voters formed, led by Bertie Ellis.

Dayton Trailblazers in Women's History...

1927—Josephine and Hermene Schwarz (sisters) founded the Dayton Ballet.

1929—Dora B. Rice became Dayton's first black policewoman.

1932—Mabel Evans first African American woman to serve on the Dayton YWCA Board of Directors

1942—Charity Adams Earley was the first black woman to become an officer in the Women's Army Auxiliary Corps in WWII.

1947—Leila Frances was the first black real estate agent in Dayton, selling homes to black families.

1950s—Edythe Lewis was Dayton's first black radio show host, named "Delilah."

1957—Marie Aull donated 70 acres to become the Aullwood Audubon Center.

1959—Virginia Kettering was Dayton's leading philanthropist and patron of the arts. "Mrs. K" as she was affectionately called, had a clear vision of what was needed in Dayton and she worked tirelessly to "light fire" under other members of the community.

1966—Clara Weisenborn was elected to the Ohio Senate and became the first female to chair a committee. She co-sponsored a bill that helped found Wright State University.

1967—Jeraldyne Blunden founded Dayton Contemporary Dance Company (DCDC).

1970—Margaret Peters, one of Dayton's foremost historians of black history and educator, published *Ebony Book of Black Achievement*.

1973—Gail Levin was appointed Dayton City Commissioner, becoming the first female to hold that position.

1976—Paula MacIlwaine was the first woman elected to Montgomery County Commissioner.

1979—Jeanne Comer founded the Dayton chapter of the Friendship Force.

1979—Alice McCollum was the first female and African American elected to Montgomery County Probate Courte Judge.

1980—Erma Bombeck was nominated to the Ohio Women's Hall of Fame for her humorous column in Dayton Daily News.

1983—Mariwyn Heath was nominated to the Ohio Women's Hall of Fame for her advocacy and work to pass the Equal Rights Amendment for women.

Dayton Trailblazers in Women's History...

1984—Yvonne Walker Taylor became the first female President of Wilberforce University.

1985—Lois Anna Barr Cook was inducted to Ohio Women's Hall of Fame for her work as a pioneering science educator.

1986—Margaret Andrew was nominated to the Ohio Women's Hall of Fame as a pioneer for women in science and technology.

1987—Sarah E. Harris was the first black woman elected to Montgomery County Treasurer.

1991—Idotha "Bootsie" Neal became the first black woman elected to the Dayton City Commission.

1994—Rhine McLin became the first black woman elected to the Ohio Senate.

1995—Minnie Fells Johnson became the first African American and female Executive Director of the Greater Dayton Regional Transit Authority (RTA).

1997—Norma Ross became the president of the Bob Ross Auto Dealership. Norma was the only black woman in the world to own a Mercedes-Benz franchise, and the only black woman to own a Buick and GMC franchise in Ohio. Her daughter, Jenell R. Ross, now owns the company, carrying on this distinction.

1999—Sharon Rab founded Dayton Literary Peace Prize.

2001—1999—Rhine McLin became the first black female mayor of Dayton.

2000—Margaret Kruckemeyer was the first female to serve on the State Board of Trustees of the Ohio Division of the American Cancer Society.

2012—Dr. Cynthia Jackson Hammond became the first female President of Central State University in its 125-year history.

2014—Nannette "Nan" Whaley is the current mayor of Dayton. She was one of the youngest to hold a commission seat at 29 years of age.

2017—Dr. Shirley Stallworth became the first African-American President of the College Women's Club of Dayton, Ohio, since its formation in 1907.

2018—Jill Dietrich became the first female director of the Dayton Veterans Affairs Medical Center.

Part Four
Test Your Knowledge

Essay Questions

Pick one of the following "Test Your Knowledge" activities and use a separate sheet of paper or you might use your phone aps or computer.

Dayton, Ohio Women Did it First!

1. Choose one of the women in this book that inspires you. Create a "comic style" story about the impact this women has had on your community, women you know, or on you! You might choose your favorite comic TV character or one of your favorite action figures to tell your story!. You could even draw your character! Which of these women did the most important thing in your opinion? Write a short essay explaining why.

2. Look at the "Dayton Ohio Women Did it First!". List and pick the one you think is most important. Write a short essay about why you chose this one.

3. Did you know that you are just as capable of accomplishing great things as these women have done? Choose a women whose impact you think made a difference. Now think about how YOU would like to make an impact like the woman you chose. How do you think being a male or female changes how you do it? Write an essay on a sheet of paper or use your computer to tell about the how you would make an impact.

NOTES:

_____
_____
_____
_____
_____
_____
_____
_____
_____
_____

Fill in the Blank

1) _____ established what today is called the Bookmobile.

2) Mary Davies Steele wrote: "_____ from itself is the happy heart."

3) The first two women physicians in Dayton were

_____.

4) In 1920, the _____ to the Constitution was passed which permitted American women the right to vote.

5) _____was elected as the first President of the Dayton Federation.

6) Emma L. Miller was the first woman in US history to be laid to rest with

_____.

7) The first African American women's organization was called the

_____.

8) Hallie Q. Brown became the first black woman to earn a _____ from Wilberforce University

9) _____ founded the Dayton Contemporary Dance Company (DCDC.).

10) Josephine and Hermene Schwarz opened what was to become the

_____.

11) _____ founded the Dayton Literary Peace Prize.

12) Rhine McLin became the first black woman to be _____.

13) _____ was nominated to the Ohio Women's Hall of Fame as a pioneer for women in science and technology.

14) In 1914, Annie McCully became Dayton's _____.

15) _____ was Dayton's first black Red Cross nurse and helped found Dayton's first YWCA for black women.

16) In _____, the Dayton Woman Suffrage Association of Montgomery County was formed and led by _____.

1. Electra C. Doren, 2. The heart at leisure, 3. Dr. Gertrude Felker, 4. 19th Amendment, 5. Marie J. Kumler, 6. full military honors, 7. "The Colored Reading Room" 8. Master of Science Degree, 9. Jeraldyne Blunden, 10. Dayton Ballet, 11. Sharon Rab, 12. elected to the Ohio Senate, 13. Margaret Andrew, 14. first policewoman, 15. Jewelia Higgins 16. 1912, Jesse Leech Davisson

Women Influence Fashion

1916 1920 1925 1930 1935 1940

1945 1950 1955 1960 1965 1970

1975 1980 1985 1990 1995 2000

2005 2010 2015 Today...

Word Search

Circle the words below backward, forward, vertically, horizontally or diagonally.

```
D W Q N H K Q N W O R B E I L L A H O
G S S A U J A S E T R E D B I B N M K
E T S T H L Z D E Y Y Y U J T L L M P
Y N F I Y L S F T N I L C M E N I H R
Z E G O J L Z S E H W A S D R Q W S B
Y M M N K D L D L J S M Q F A T Y O U
O D N A G F C U E F W I D V R R U I L
P N U L B G V R C G A N C B Y E J U C
Q E L C N C D Y T C A N V C C R K H S
E M M A M V F U R S M I C X L E L N N
R A N S R S E I A D E E H E U T K G A
R H V H E W E I D T Z S I R B T M S M
B T S R W E R P O V X T J N L E M A O
C N S E S W T V R B C A K T N G J Z W
V E K G D T H O E N D N J Y L A T D N
U E L I F T W C N E F L L U O R R S O
I T N S G H S I R R G E M I U F F S T
P N M T H R C Q U A F Y I P Y F G H Y
L I O E H R C U I T M G O O Y U H F A
K N O R M A R O S S U G P N X S V B D
R E Y E M E K C U R K T E R A G R A M
```

Annie McCully

Dayton Woman's Club

Electra Doren

Hallie Brown

Literary Club

March

Margaret Kruckemeyer

Minnie Stanley

National Cash Register

Nineteenth Amendment

Norma Ross

Rhine McLin

Suffragette

Vote

NOTES